EDGE
BOOKS™

TIGERS

BIG CATS

BY CLAUDETTE HEGEL

Consultant: Christina Simmons
San Diego Zoo Global
San Diego, California

CAPSTONE PRESS
a capstone imprint

Edge Books are published by Capstone Press,
1710 Roe Crest Drive, North Mankato, Minnesota 56003.
www.capstonepub.com

 Books published by Capstone Press are manufactured with paper
containing at least 10 percent post-consumer waste.

Library of Congress Cataloging-in-Publication Data
Hegel, Claudette.
   Tigers / by Claudette Hegel Edge Books.
      p. cm. — (Edge books: big cats)
   Includes bibliographical references and index.
   ISBN 978-1-4296-7646-5 (library binding)
   1. Tiger—Juvenile literature. I. Title.
   QL737.C23H44 2012
   599.756—dc23   2011021016

Summary: "Describes the history, physical features, and habitat of tigers"
—Provided by publisher.

Editorial Credits
Brenda Haugen, editor; Kyle Grenz, designer; Svetlana Zhurkin,
      media researcher; Laura Manthe, production specialist

Photo Credits
Alamy: blickwinkel, 5, Alastair Lloyd, 6, Natural Visions, 15, Frans Lanting
Studio, 19, Juniors Bildarchiv, 21; Creatas, 1, 13, 28; Digital Stock, 29; Digital
Vision, 4; Dreamstime: Elshaneo, 9, Sudhir Mishra, 23 (top), Helen E. Grose,
24; iStockphoto: Jameson Weston, cover; National Geographic Stock: Minden
Pictures/Zhinong Xi, 26; Nature Picture Library: Anup Shah, 16; Shutterstock:
Ammit, 20, Chris Sargent, 12, Dennis Donohue, 10, Helen E. Grose, 14, Jirsak,
18, Kitch Bain, 7, M. Robbemont, 23 (bottom), Martin Dallaire, 25, Olga
Bogatyrenko, 22, Petr Mašek, 11, Stanislav Eduardovich Petrov (background),
throughout, Stephen Meese, 17, Tatiana Morozova, 27, Tiago Jorge da Silva
Estima, 8

Printed in the United States of America in Stevens Point, Wisconsin.
012013   007152R

TABLE OF CONTENTS

Chapter 1

THE REAL KING OF THE JUNGLE

Some people call the lion the king of the jungle, but lions don't live in jungles. Some tigers do live in jungles. Since tigers have no **predators** other than people, tigers really are the kings of the jungle.

Tigers live in a variety of **habitats**. Tigers live in forests, swamps, and rocky areas. Tigers thrive where they have enough water, food, and places to hide while hunting.

predator—an animal that hunts other animals for food

habitat—the natural place and conditions in which an animal or plant lives

All wild tigers live in Asia. Most types of tigers live in warm areas. Only Siberian, or Amur, tigers live in areas that have cold winters.

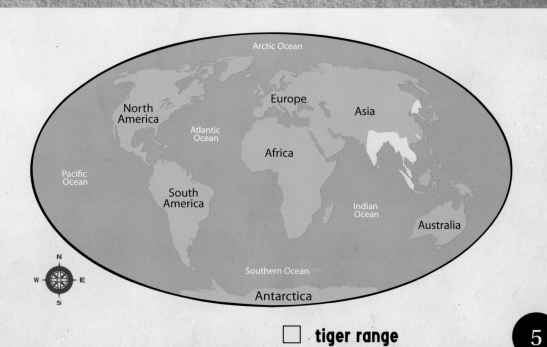

☐ tiger range

A TIGER'S STRIPES AND COAT

The tiger is the only big cat with stripes. The stripes help it blend in with its surroundings. No two tigers have the same pattern of stripes. Most tigers have more than 100 stripes. A few tigers have been born without stripes, but this is very rare.

White Tigers

White tigers are not a separate **species**. They are regular tigers born with a white coat. About one of every 10,000 tigers born is white. These cats have brown or gray stripes. They have pink noses and blue eyes.

White tigers usually grow faster than other tigers. White tigers are usually larger too. This trait may help them catch **prey**, because white tigers don't blend in with their surroundings like other tigers do.

Most white tigers in zoos are descended from a white tiger named Mohan. Because white tigers are unusual, they are among the most popular animals in zoos.

A tiger's coat is often yellow to red-brown. The stripes may be black, brown, or gray. The skin under a tiger's fur also has stripes. A tiger's white underside doesn't have stripes. Tigers also have white spots on the backs of their ears.

species—a group of animals or plants that share common characteristics

Big Cat Fact

Did you ever see what looks like a letter on a tiger's forehead? These forehead stripes look like the letter "I" with an extra line through the center. This mark is called a wang, meaning "king."

SIZE

Male tigers have a ruff of hair around their faces. This ruff isn't as noticeable as a lion's mane. Although lions have larger manes, tigers have larger bodies. Tigers are the biggest cats. An adult tiger's head and body may be more than 10 feet (3 meters) long. Its tail may be 3 feet (1 m) long. An adult tiger is about 3 feet (1 m) tall at the shoulder. Tigers can weigh as much as 675 pounds (306 kilograms).

Size Comparison Chart

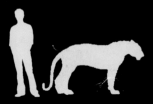

The average height of an American male is 5 feet, 10 inches (178 centimeters).

ON THE MOVE

A tiger's strong body helps it make quick rushes and long leaps. Tigers can run 40 miles (64 kilometers) per hour for short distances. They can jump up to 33 feet (10 m) in one leap. Long tails help tigers keep their balance.

Big Cat Fact

A group of tigers is called an ambush or a streak.

dewclaw

FANCY FEET

A tiger has big, sharp, **retractable** claws on powerful paws. Tigers have four toes on each paw. They also have a **dewclaw** on each of their front paws. Pads on the bottom of their feet help tigers walk quietly.

retractable—able to be drawn in from an extended position

dewclaw—an extra toe with a claw found higher up than other toes on a tiger's front paw

11

A TIGER'S HEAD

It's hard to catch a tiger off guard. Tigers hear more than three times as well as people do. They also have great eyesight. At the back of each of a tiger's large, round eyes is a mirror-like structure. Light bounces off the structure, and the structure creates more light. The added brightness allows a tiger to see six times better than people do at night. During the day, people see a little more clearly than tigers.

Tigers have whiskers on their cheeks, above their eyes, and around their **muzzles**. Whiskers help the big cats feel things around them.

Strong jaws and 30 huge, sharp teeth help a tiger kill and eat its prey. A tiger's longest teeth are almost half as long as an unsharpened pencil.

Tigers have rough tongues. They use their tongues to eat, show affection to other tigers, and groom themselves.

muzzle–an animal's nose, mouth, and jaw

Chapter 2

THE THRILL OF THE HUNT

Tigers are **carnivores**. Deer and wild boars are a tiger's favorite prey. Tigers also eat birds, snakes, fish, bugs, and other animals. Even an elephant or rhino calf may become a tiger's dinner.

A tiger can eat about 40 pounds (18 kg) of food at one meal. After a big meal, a tiger may not eat for the next few days.

14   **carnivore**–an animal that eats only meat

Big Cat Fact

Sometimes tigers take kills away from other animals instead of hunting for themselves.

HOW TIGERS HUNT

Most tigers hunt alone. A tiger's sharp ears hear the rustle of prey. A tiger's keen eyesight helps it spot its next meal.

Tigers crouch in tall grass to hide from prey. A tiger may follow its prey for 20 or 30 minutes. No sound comes from a tiger's footsteps.

The tiger moves closer, approaching its prey from the side or back. At the right time, the big cat pounces. The tiger's heavy body, strong legs, and sharp claws force the prey to the ground. A tiger often kills a small animal by breaking its neck or ripping out its throat. A tiger may hold on to a large animal's neck until it quits breathing.

15

LIMITED SUCCESS

Tigers are not always successful on their hunts.
A tiger makes a kill only once every 10 to 20 tries.
The prey often escapes. Prey that sees a leaping tiger
often can jump away from the attack. Large animals
may shake off a tiger. Sometimes big, strong prey
can hurt or even kill a tiger.

AFTER THE KILL

Tigers often carry or drag their kills to safe places before eating. A tiger starts eating at an animal's rump. A tiger's sharp incisor teeth work like knives slicing off the meat. Premolar and molar teeth help a tiger tear and chew meat. A tiger's rough tongue scrapes the bones for any leftover meat.

Most of the time, a tiger saves the rest of an animal for future meals. Large prey can feed a tiger for several meals. Sometimes tigers share a large kill with other tigers.

A tiger covers its leftovers with grass and dirt to keep other animals from eating the meat. A tiger goes back to the hiding spot to eat the next several days. The big cat eats the meat even if it spoils.

Big Cat Fact

A female tiger without cubs makes a kill about every eight days. A female with cubs catches prey about every five or six days.

17

Chapter 3

DAILY LIFE

Do you like to jump in the water on a hot day? Tigers do. Female tigers teach their cubs to go into water. You may swim with a friend, but tigers are usually alone. The only time tigers aren't alone is when they are mating or caring for their young.

That doesn't mean tigers don't communicate. Tigers make about 50 sounds, including purring almost like a house cat. You can hear a tiger roar 2 miles (3.2 km) away. A tiger may growl, snarl, or hiss at other animals in its **territory**.

territory—an area of land that an animal claims as its own to live in

TIGER TERRITORY

How do you know where a tiger's territory is? Tigers mark the edges of their territories in many ways. Sometimes tigers leave claw marks on tree trunks. They may scrape their back feet across the ground to mark the edges of their territories. Tigers also spray smelly urine onto trees, bushes, and other areas. Females use this kind of **scent marking** to attract mates. Males use scent marking to warn other males to stay out of their territories.

scent marking—leaving a smell to warn other animals to stay away or as a mating signal

MATING

Female tigers call to males when they want to mate. Tigers usually mate during cooler months.

When a male and female meet, they circle each other and growl. The female may even run away with the male chasing after her. Finally the tigers mate. They spend several days together. Then the male leaves, but he may be back after the cubs are born.

About 100 days after mating, the female finds a cave, hollow tree, or another safe place near water and prey. She uses grass to make a soft area where her cubs are born.

TIGER CUBS

A tiger's litter may include up to seven cubs. Most litters have about three cubs. One or more cubs often die at birth.

A newborn cub weighs about 2.5 pounds (1 kg). A cub's eyes are not open right away. Newborn cubs are helpless.

Cubs live only on their mother's milk for six to eight weeks. Then their mother starts sharing her kills with them. Sometimes the father tiger also shares a kill with his cubs. The cubs continue drinking their mother's milk until they are 3 to 6 months old.

GROWING CUBS

Tiger cubs play the way house cats do. Play is part of their mother's hunting lessons.

Tigers start making their own kills when they are about 18 months old. During this time, the tiger family may kill more prey than it can eat. The young tigers sometimes leave their mother soon afterward. Other cubs may stay with their mothers until they are up to 3 years old. Young tigers often leave when their mother starts sharing her kills with a new litter of cubs.

Big Cat Fact

Tigers sometimes hunt as families, but more often they hunt alone. By hunting alone, a tiger has a better chance of sneaking up on prey. Prey is more likely to see or hear a group of tigers and escape.

Wild tigers usually live about 8 to 10 years. With enough prey, tigers may live 15 years or more in the wild. Zoo tigers can live 20 years or more.

Chapter 4

SAVE THE TIGERS

Just 100 years ago, about 100,000 tigers lived in the wild. Today only about 3,200 wild tigers still exist.

Big Cat Fact

A 2004 survey of 50,000 people in 73 countries showed that tigers are people's favorite animals. Dogs ranked second, and dolphins were third.

Many kinds of tigers are now **extinct**. Only six types of tigers remain, and they are all **endangered**. They are the Bengal, Indo-Chinese, Malayan, Siberian, South China, and Sumatran tigers.

The Siberian tiger was almost extinct in the 1940s. People worked to save the tigers, and their numbers grew.

extinct—no longer living; an extinct animal is one that has died out, with no more of its kind

endangered—at risk of dying out

25

Big Cat Fact

A poacher may get more than $100,000 for one tiger.
Some people will pay a high price for a tiger skin rug or coat.

WHY TIGERS ARE ENDANGERED

The number of tigers is dropping for many reasons. People move near tigers and take away their habitats and prey. Not as many tigers can live in a smaller area.

Tigers sometimes kill farm animals and attack people. In the 1950s and 1960s, the Chinese government ordered tigers shot or poisoned. Now scientists aren't sure if South China tigers exist anymore in the wild. A few of the tigers still live in zoos.

Some people kill tigers, even though it is against the law. These people are called poachers. Some poachers kill tigers for fun. Other poachers sell tigers. Others use a tiger's body parts for medicine they think will cure illnesses. Even though the medicines don't work, people still buy them. And poachers will keep killing tigers as long as they make money.

Tiger Farms

A tiger farm is a place where tigers live in cages or fenced areas the way cattle do on ranches. Most tiger farms charge a fee for people to see the tigers. Some farms have shows with trained tigers that perform tricks. Farmers often sell parts of tigers that die on the farms.

Many tiger protection groups want to stop tiger farming. They say people need to stop using tiger parts for anything. The groups believe that is the best way to stop poachers from killing the big cats.

A rescued tiger cub is fed from a bottle.

SAVING TIGERS

Killing tigers has been a crime since the 1970s. Even those who don't kill tigers may threaten the big cats' survival. For example, if hunters kill tigers' prey, the big cats starve.

Some countries set up tiger **reserves** to save tiger habitat. The United States and many other countries help pay for the reserves.

Some zoos have tiger breeding programs. But tigers born and raised in captivity cannot live in the wild. Tigers that are used to people can be dangerous if released into the wild.

Saving tigers is important. Nature needs tigers to stay in balance. Without tigers, prey animals may become too plentiful. Many prey animals would starve to death as their food becomes scarce. If we save tigers now, people in the future will still have these majestic animals to enjoy.

GLOSSARY

carnivore (KAHR-nuh-vohr)—an animal that eats only meat

dewclaw (DOO-klah)—an extra toe with a claw found higher up than other toes on a tiger's front paw

endangered (in-DAYN-juhrd)—at risk of dying out

extinct (ik-STINGKT)—no longer living; an extinct animal is one that has died out, with no more of its kind

habitat (HAB-uh-tat)—the natural place and conditions in which an animal or plant lives

muzzle (MUHZ-uhl)—an animal's nose, mouth, and jaw

predator (PRED-uh-tur)—an animal that hunts other animals for food

prey (PRAY)—an animal hunted by another animal for food

reserve (ri-ZURV)—land that is protected so that animals may live there safely

retractable (ri-TRAK-tuh-buhl)—able to be drawn in from an extended position

scent marking (SENT MARK-ing)—leaving a smell to warn other animals to stay away or as a mating signal

species (SPEE-sheez)—a group of animals or plants that share common characteristics

territory (TER-uh-tor-ee)—an area of land that an animal claims as its own to live in

READ MORE

Barnes, Julia. *The Secret Lives of Tigers*. The Secret Lives of Animals. Milwaukee: Gareth Stevens Pub., 2007.

Markert, Jenny. *Tigers*. New Nature Books. Mankato, Minn.: Child's World, 2008.

Smith, Lucy Sackett. *Tigers: Prowling Predators*. Mighty Mammals Series. New York: PowerKids Press, 2010.

INTERNET SITES

FactHound offers a safe, fun way to find Internet sites related to this book. All of the sites on FactHound have been researched by our staff.

Here's all you do:

Visit *www.facthound.com*

Type in this code: 9781429676465

Super-cool stuff! Check out projects, games and lots more at www.capstonekids.com

INDEX